My Extended Family Photos – Angela C. Williams

God/Love/Peace/Family/Career/Mate/Friends/Fun

I0470495

By

Angela C. Williams

My Extended Family Photos – Angela C. Williams

God/Love/Peace/Family/Career/Mate/Friends/Fun

By

Angela C. Williams

Copyright © 2015
All Rights Reserved

ISBN-13: 9781518854217
ISBN-10: 1518854214

Dedication

To My Mother Christine S. Williams, I miss her so much

50th Wedding Anniversary

of

Booker T. and Sophonia Staten

They married at the ages of 14 and 15 years. They had 8 children: 3 girls and 5 boys.

William is the best man
From left to right: David, Russell, Booker T. Jr. and Harry are pictured with their father, my grandfather; Booker T. Staten Sr.

From left to right: Deloris, Lorine and Christine, my mother; are all pictured with their mother; Sophonia Staten.

The wives of all five sons, are also pictured.
The ring bearer, flower girl and poetry reader, are grandchildren Patrick, Tenille and me, Angela.

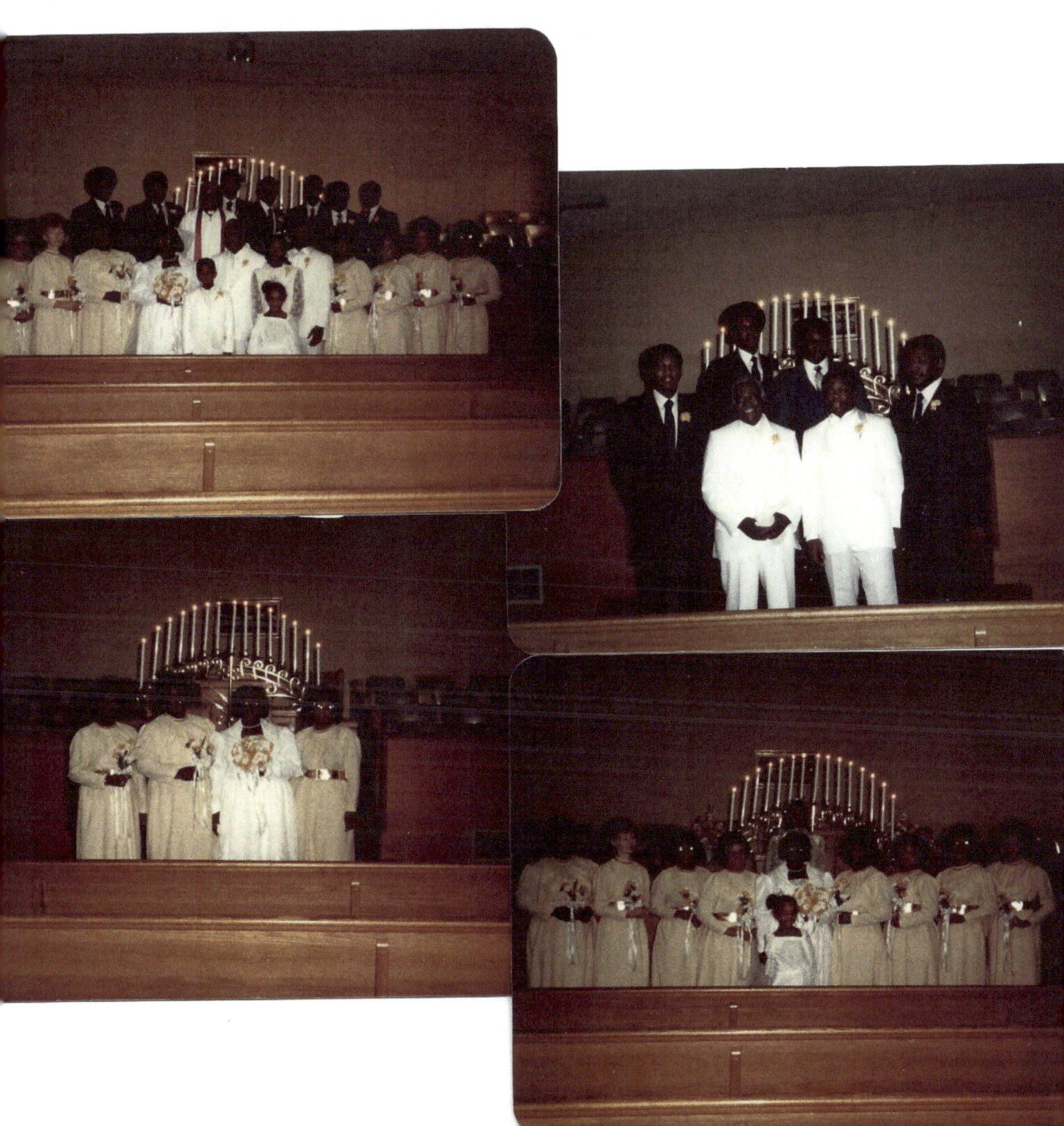

The next page:

A picture of me and my brother.

I love him very much. I think our family let him down.

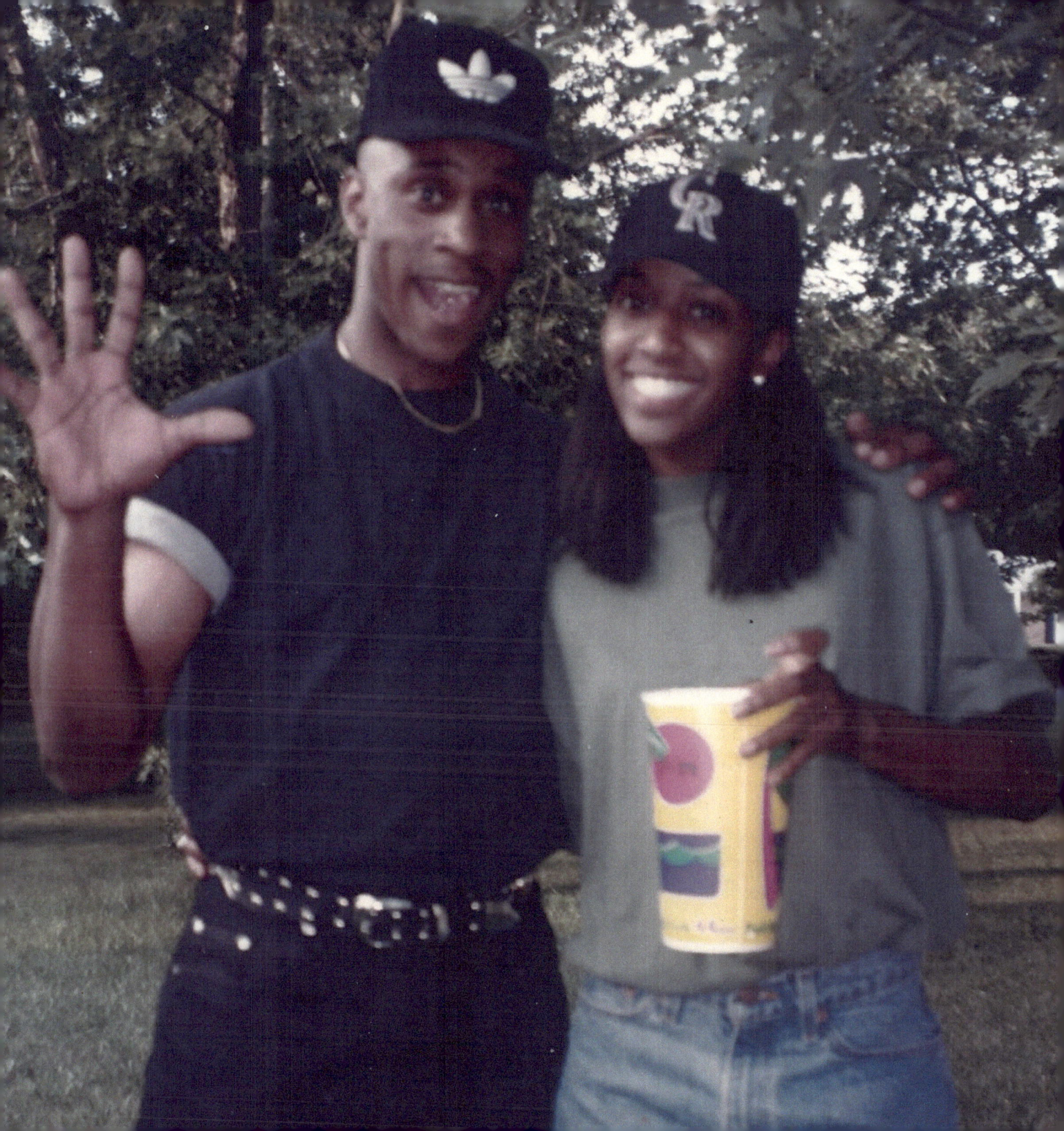

The following page is a picture of me, the author. And here you see my immediate family.

OK and there is a small picture of me when I won first runner up in the Miss Teen Pageant at age 14. Lol

My father Jerry C. Williams and my late mother Christine S. Williams.

My only child, Indigo Harper and my brothers only child, Kyle Williams are also pictured.

The 5x7 photo is my graduation picture from high school in 1991. (Angela C. Williams)

My brother is a former Marine. Carlos J. Williams (Once a Marine always a Marine).

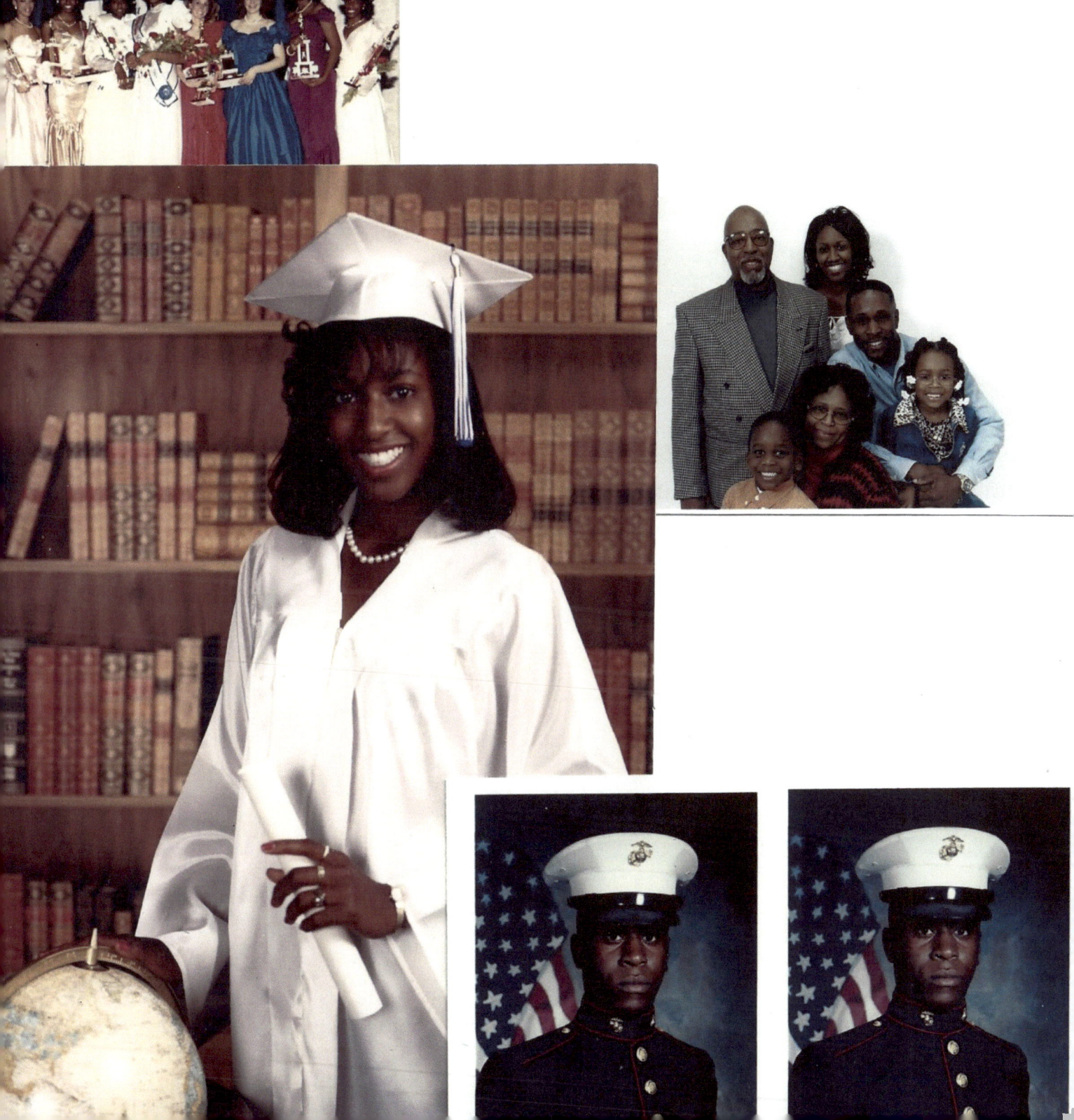

On the next page, you will see a picture of my parents and a picture of me and my daughter's father Dustin; who is also my ex-husband. My brother is also pictured with his ex-wife Sheila who is the mother of his son, Kyle.

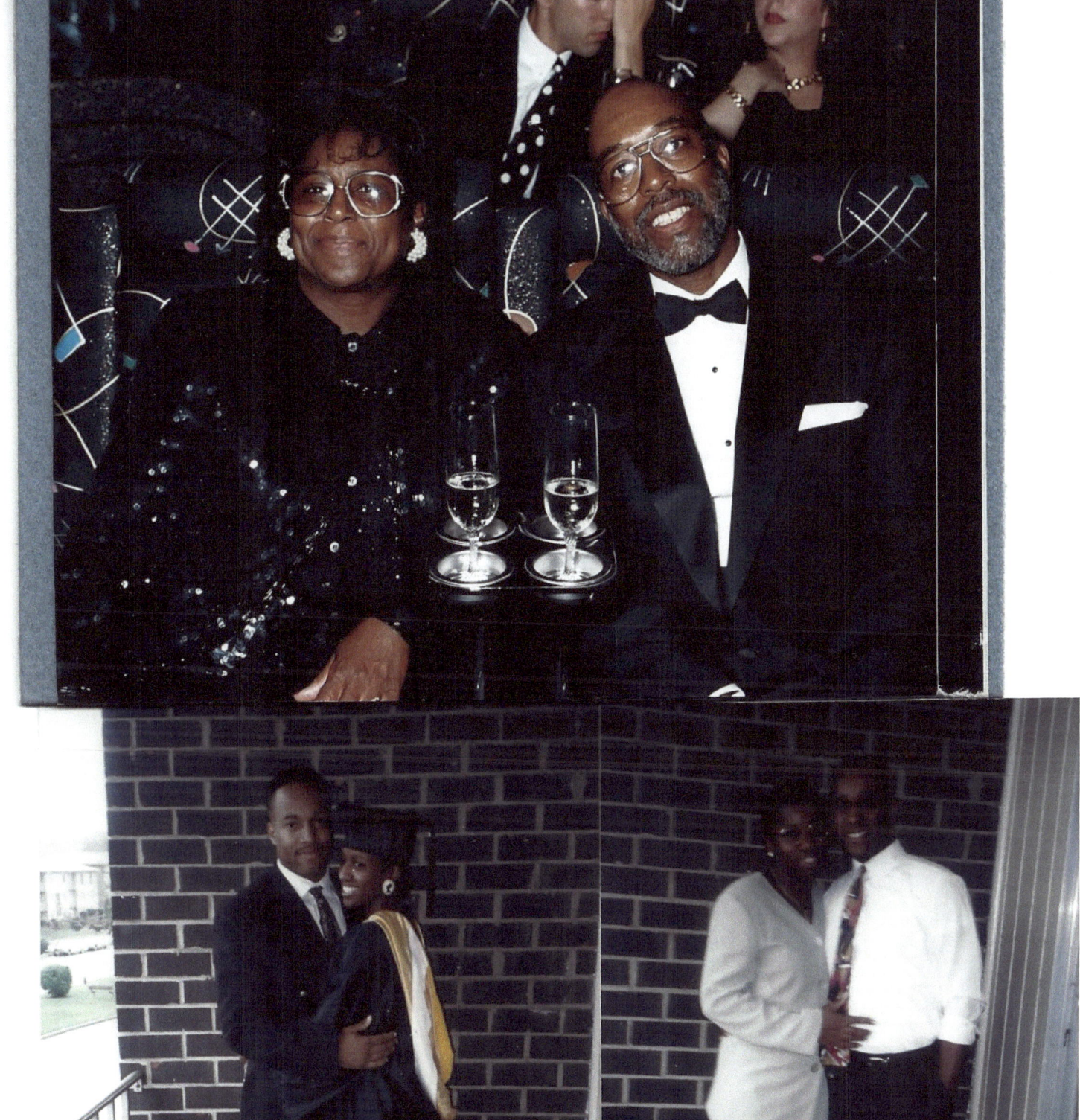

The next page is a picture of my brother and his stepson Anthony, from his marriage to Sheila. The other pictures are of my daughter's grandparents on her father's side Freddie and Sharon. Also pictured is her aunt Dallas; her father's sister. Her father is remarried to a woman named Sharon. The have three young girls: Soteria, Zoe and Selena.

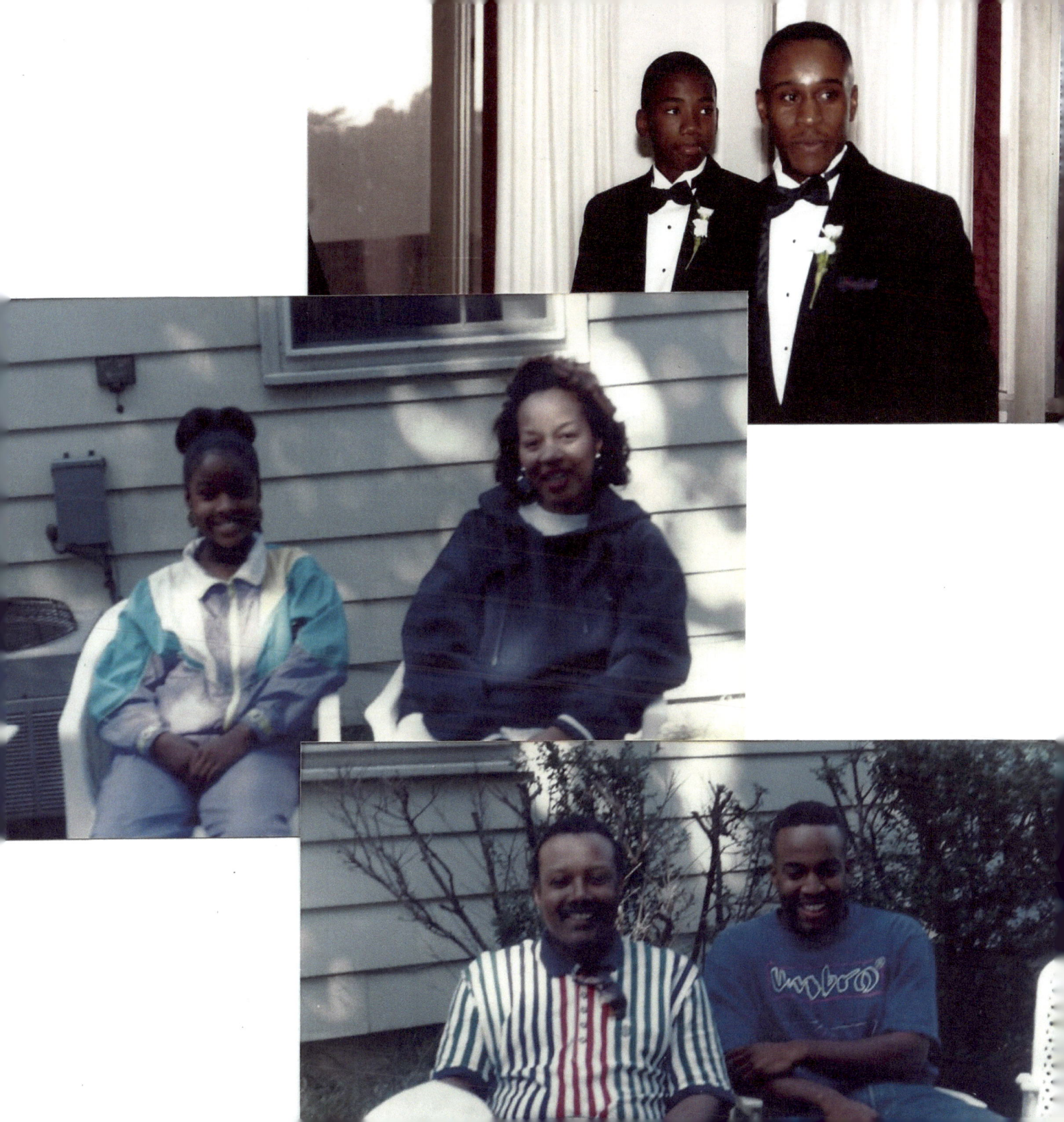

Lorine is my mother's sister. She is pictured on the next page with her three sons: Former Army Sgt. Matthew Lorenzo Pickett Sr., Former Marine Sgt. Mark Anthony Pickett and Carlton A. Pickett. Her oldest, Lorenzo is married with (three) children. He and his wife, Patty; lost their son (Matthew), a few years ago. Their children are young in this picture. He was a great kid and he would have been a great asset to society. I suppose God wanted him nearer to Him in Heaven. Danelle and Dominique are their daughters.

Her tall lighter-skinned, middle son is married with three children. They had only the one daughter during these pictures. Pictured on the next page are his wife Angela and their first daughter Lauren.

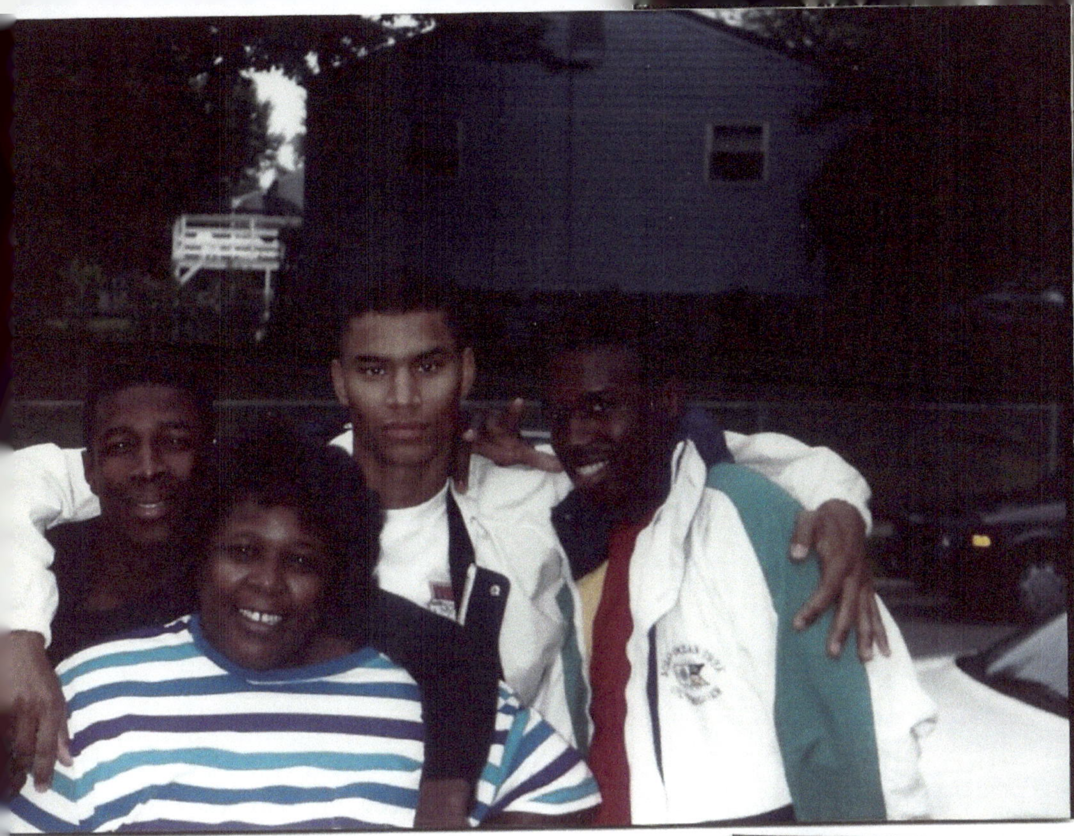

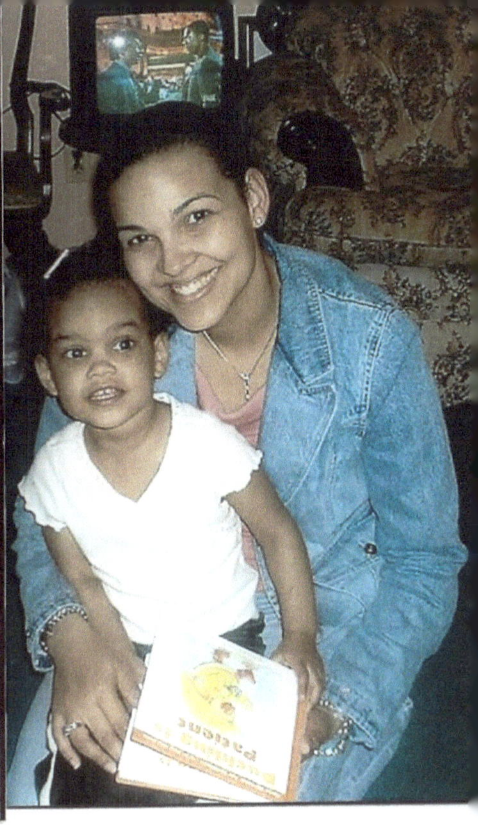

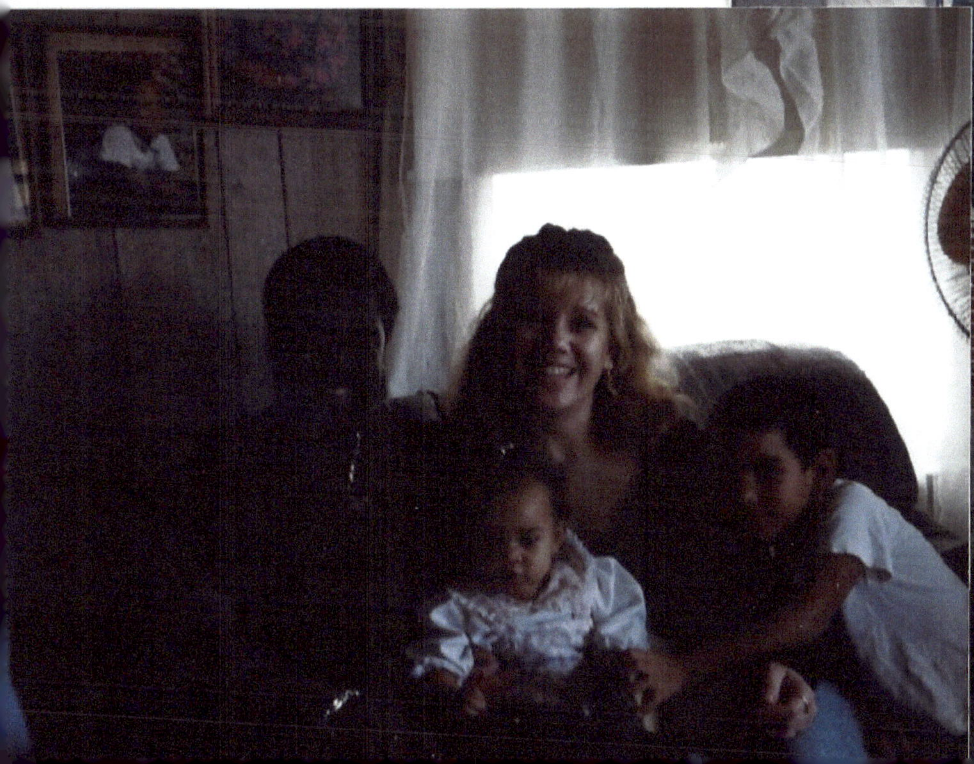

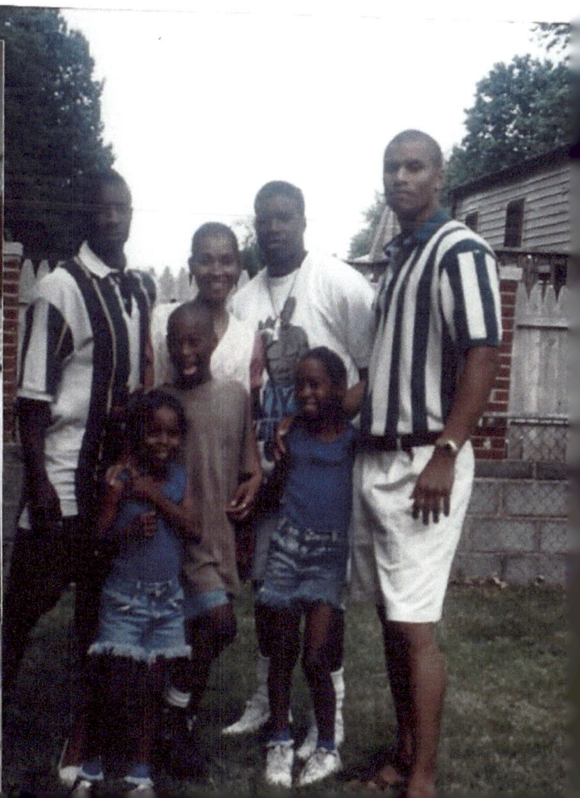

The next page holds this picture:

Her youngest son Carlton, has a child named Brittany by a woman named Kalen, whom is not pictured.
Brittany is on the upcoming page, on the left, in pink. (She now has her own baby girl). Carlton married Janice and had two girls (Kayla and Morgan), pictured on the next page, with my daughter who is holding the basketball. His stepson Devin; is young here and wearing a white tuxedo. Carlton has since remarried Jen and had 4 new children and one step child. They are not pictured.

The other two girls in pink belong to Lorines oldest son Lorenzo. Danelle, the oldest of the two, has three young girls who are not pictured: Dayanna, Denyla and Delia. Dominique is the younger. Mark and his former girlfriend Robin have an adult son named Torres, who is not pictured.

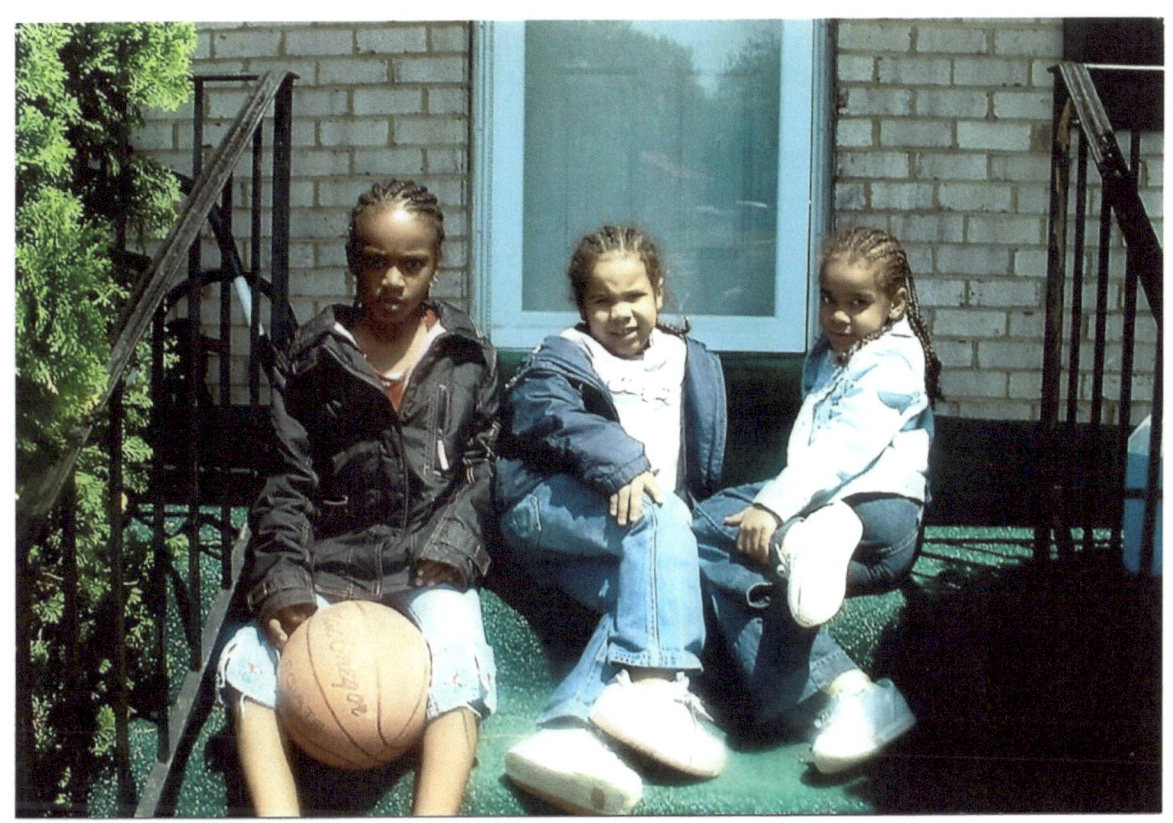

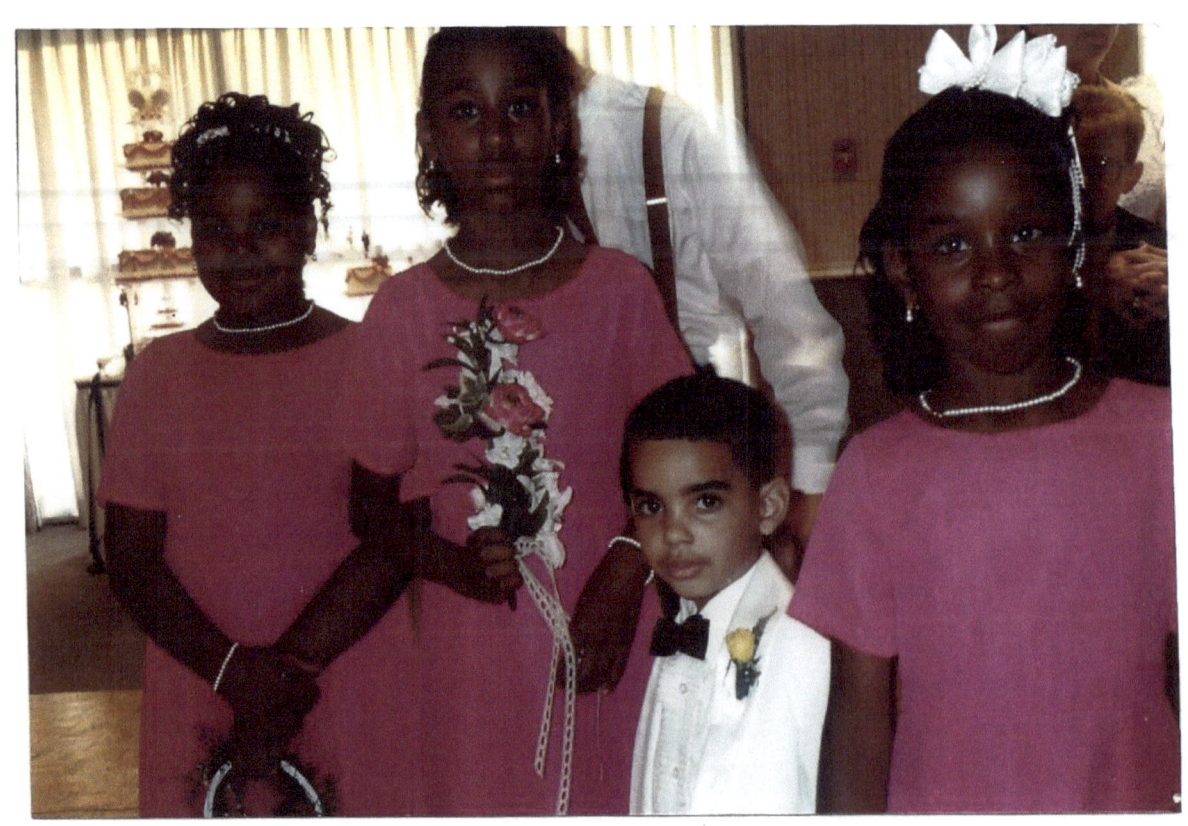

The next page has a family photo of my mother's brother David, his wife Mary and their two children; Drew and Daedre.

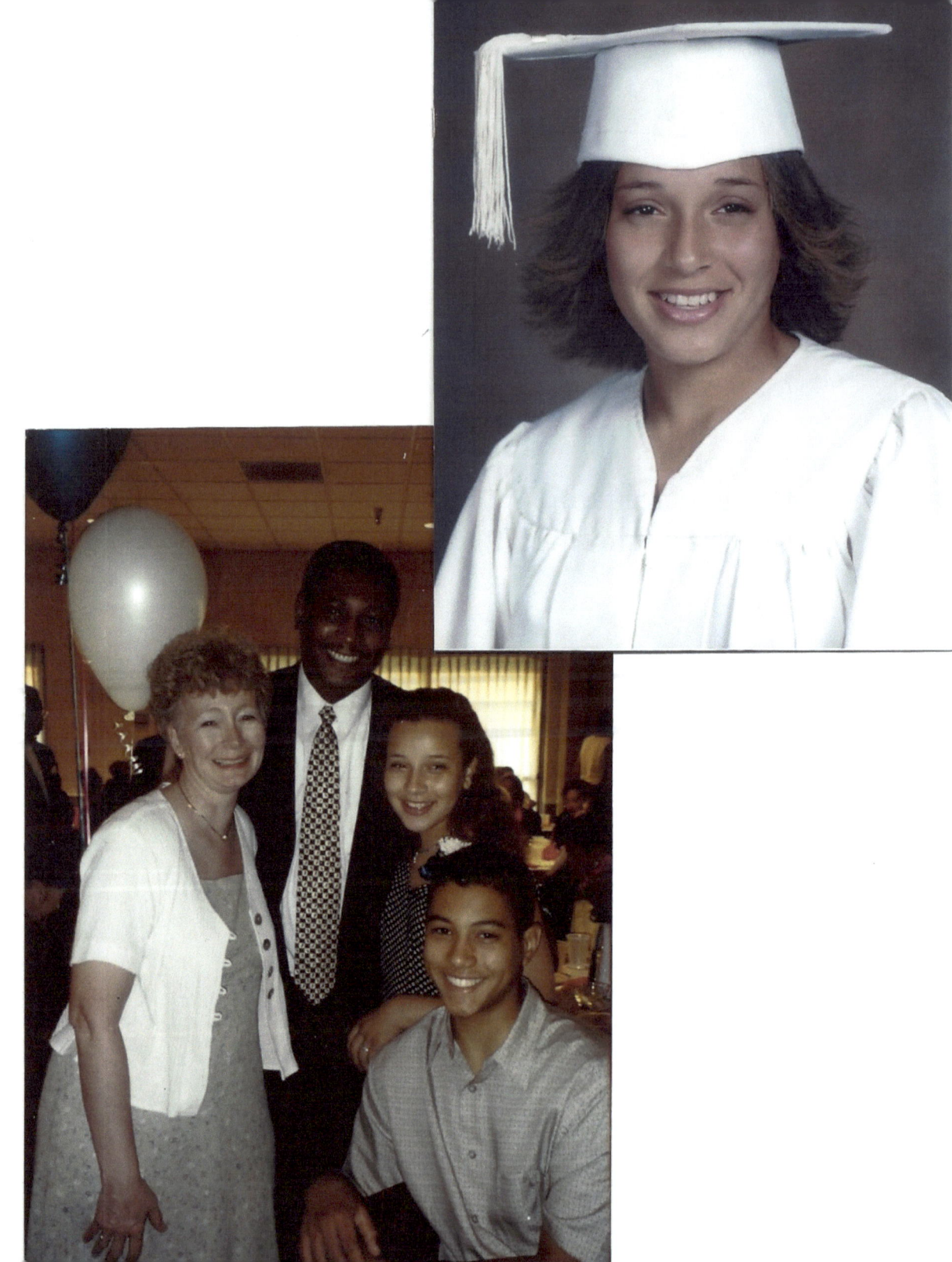

`   The next set of pictures are of my mother's brother, Booker T. Staten and his late wife Helen. The bottom picture is of their only child, Dewayne and his former wife Velicia. They have two boys; Dewayne and Dante', who are pictured next to them. Dewayne is remarried, but she is not pictured.

The picture to the right, is of my mother's youngest brother, Russell Staten and his wife Terry. They are pictured with their two daughters, Renae and Tenille. Their grandchildren are not pictured. The bottom picture is of Terry's mother.

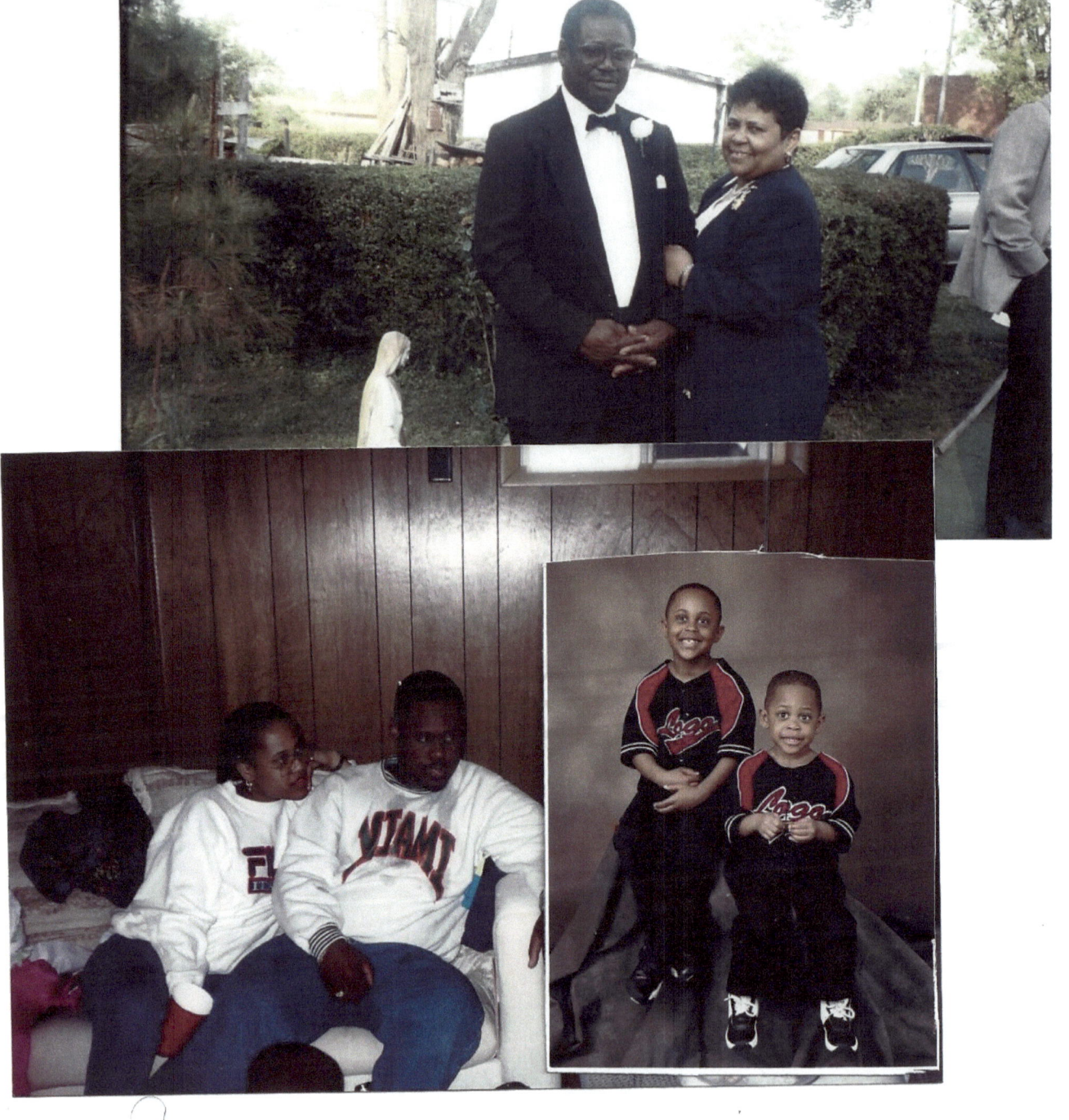

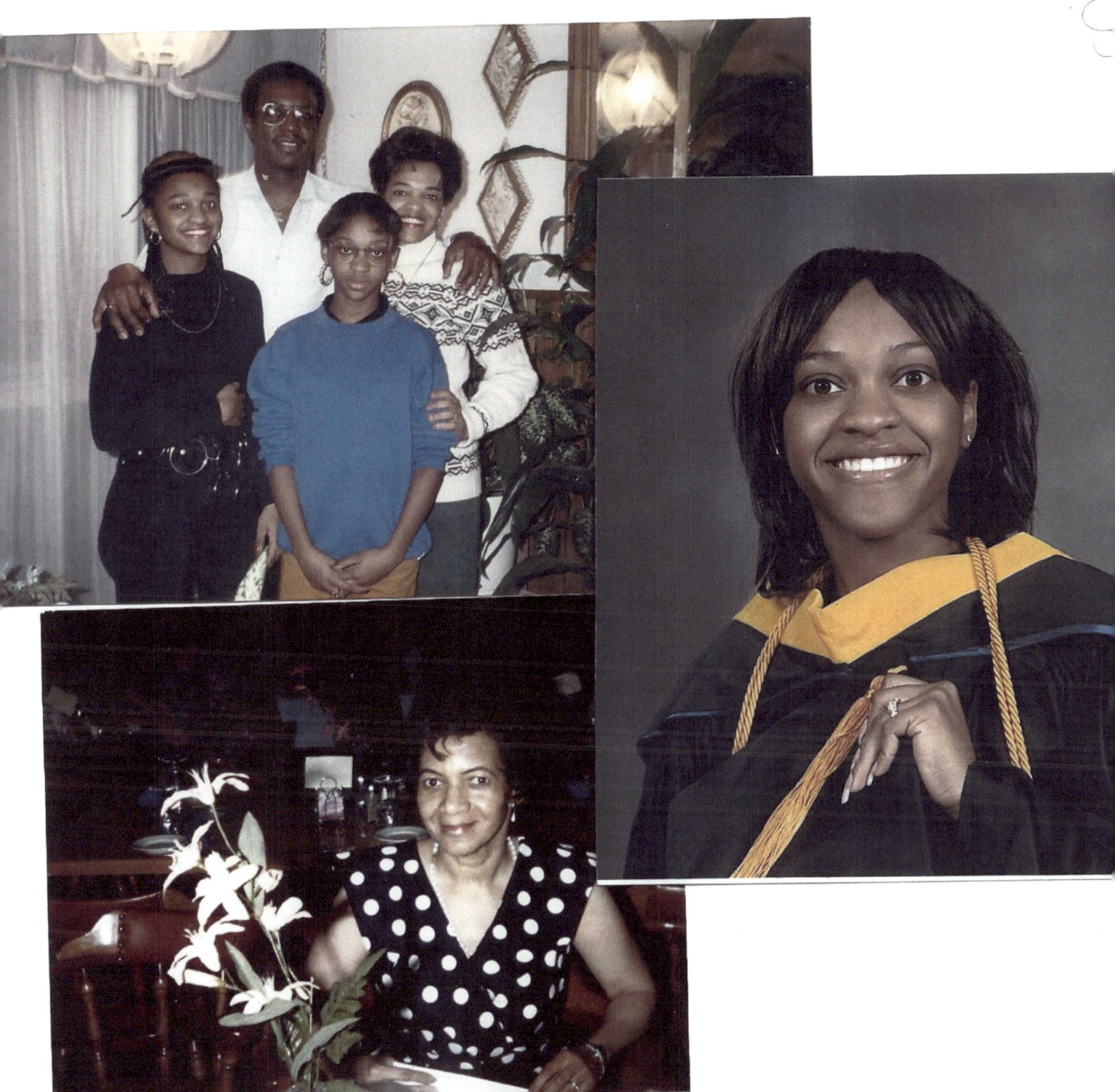

The next page is of William Staten and his first wife Elaine. There is a picture of his late daughter Sophonia and her husband. Their 5 college aged children are not pictured. His son Patrick, is sitting next to him at the table, in the bottom right corner of the bottom right picture on the page. You can see his face partially. Patrick's wife and children are not pictured.

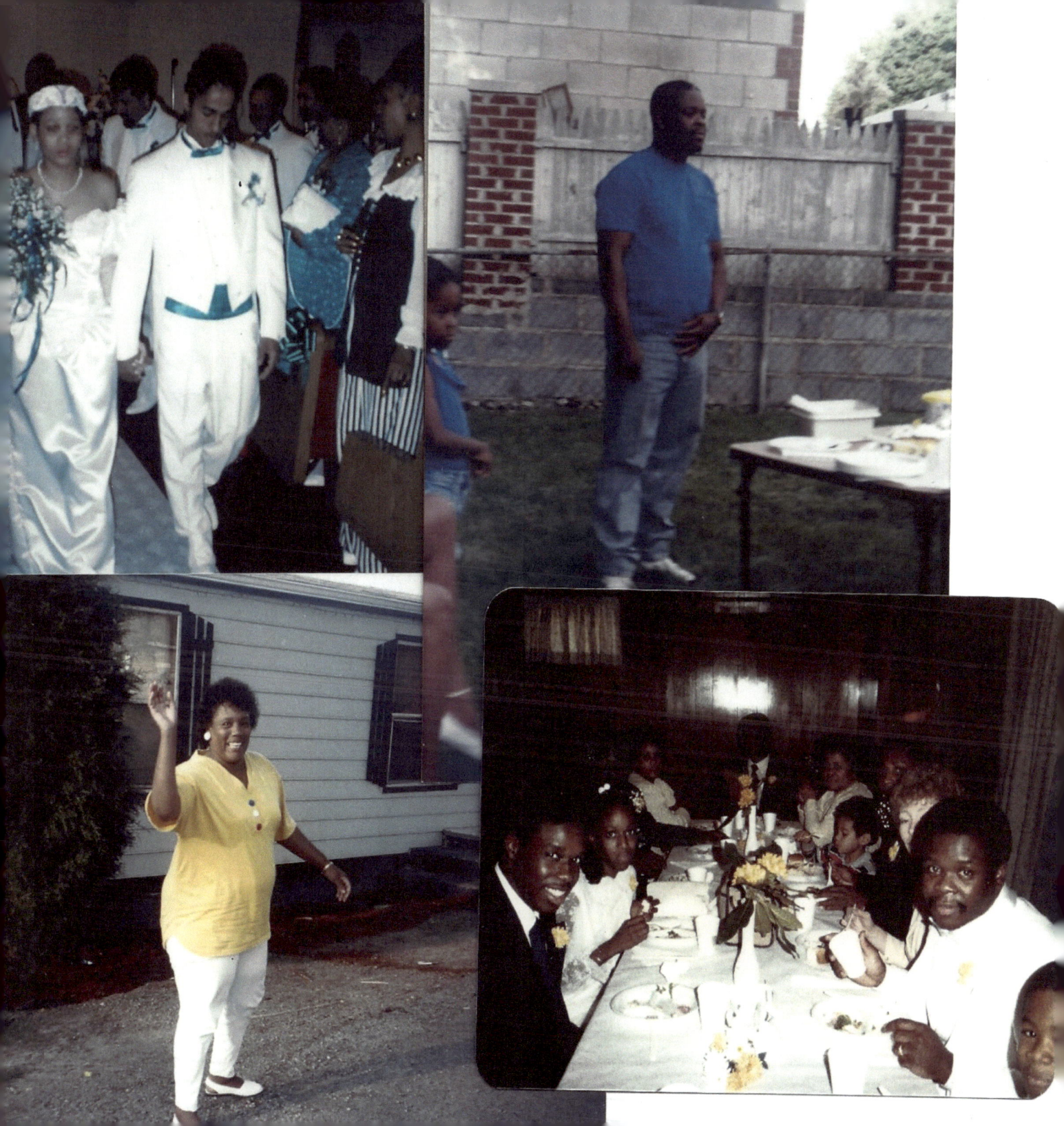

The next set of pictures is of my mother's sister Deloris and her late husband Charles. He is at the table to the far right. Their only daughter, Gwendolyn Denise, is pictured with her. One of his two other children, is pictured with her only child. (Deborah and Danae). His son Toni, is not pictured.

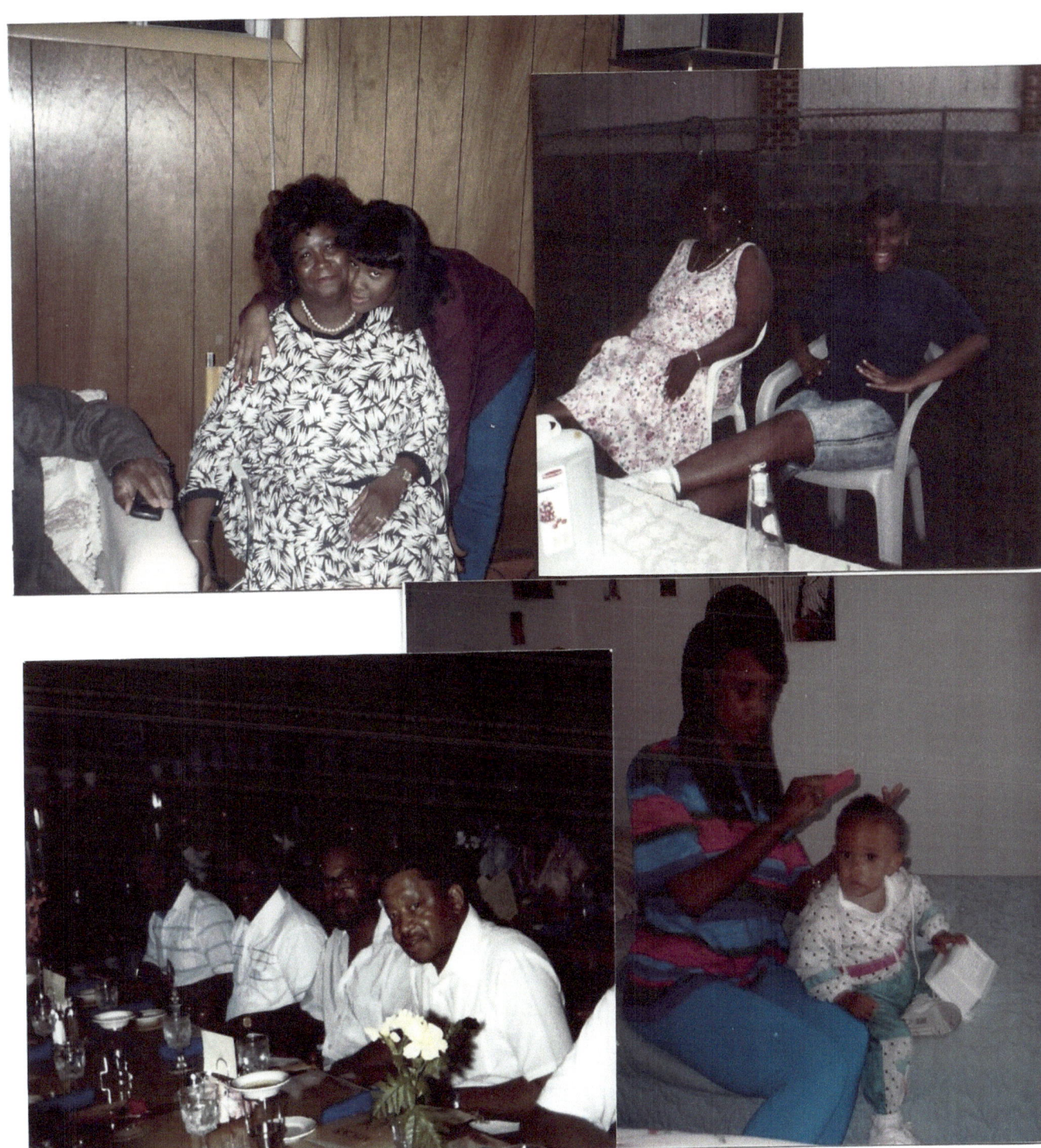

This next set of pictures is of my mother's brother, Former Air Force Sgt. Harry and his wife Mary; who is wearing glasses. They have two daughters (who are very young here); Sylvia on the left. She is married to Dorie. And Lisa who is married with two boys.

Harry and his wife lost one newborn child, many years before their two girls were born.

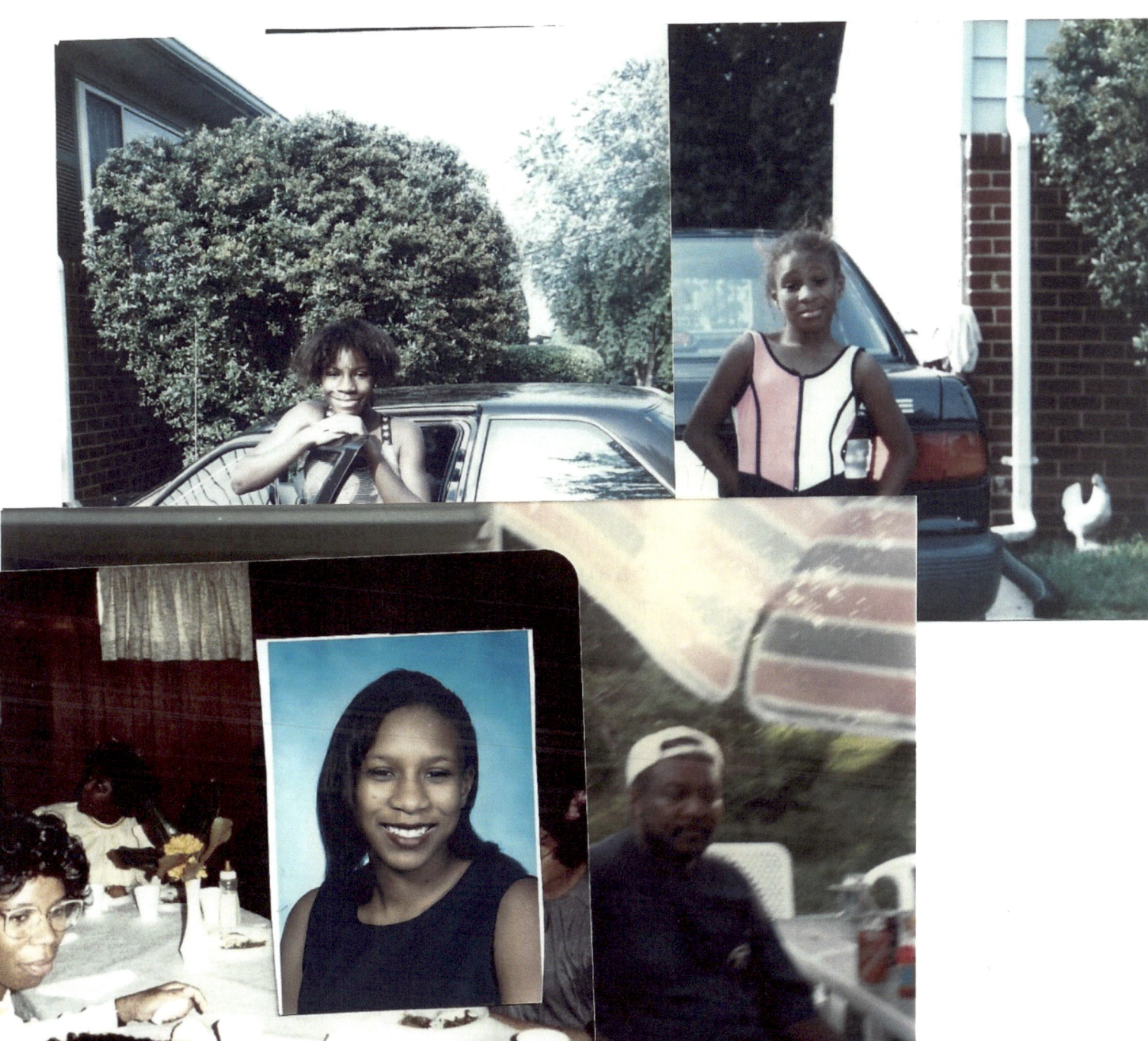

The next set of pictures are of my mother's aunt Alice with the two guys leaning on her shoulder and Uncle George with the white hair.
Her cousin Julia, sipping her drink (who is recently married). And Julia's sister, Vivian. Vivian's husband is sitting at the far end of the table, with her to his right. Their daughter Katrina is not pictured, but has since grown up and married.

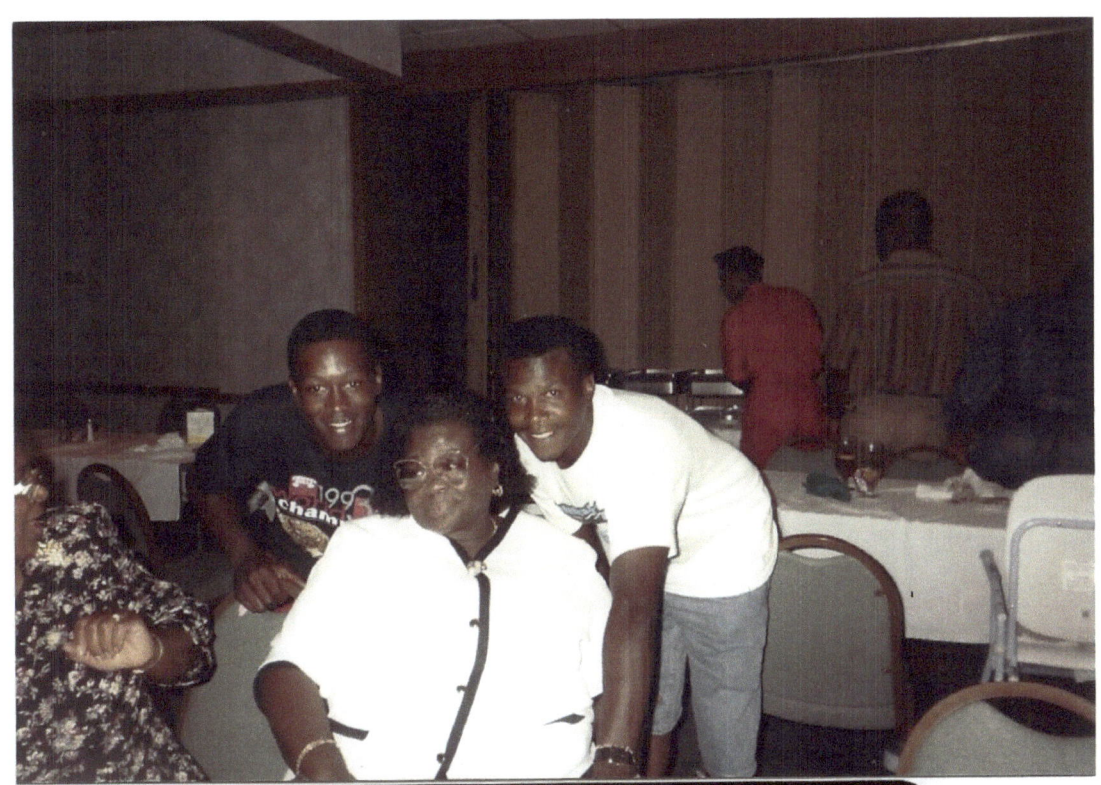

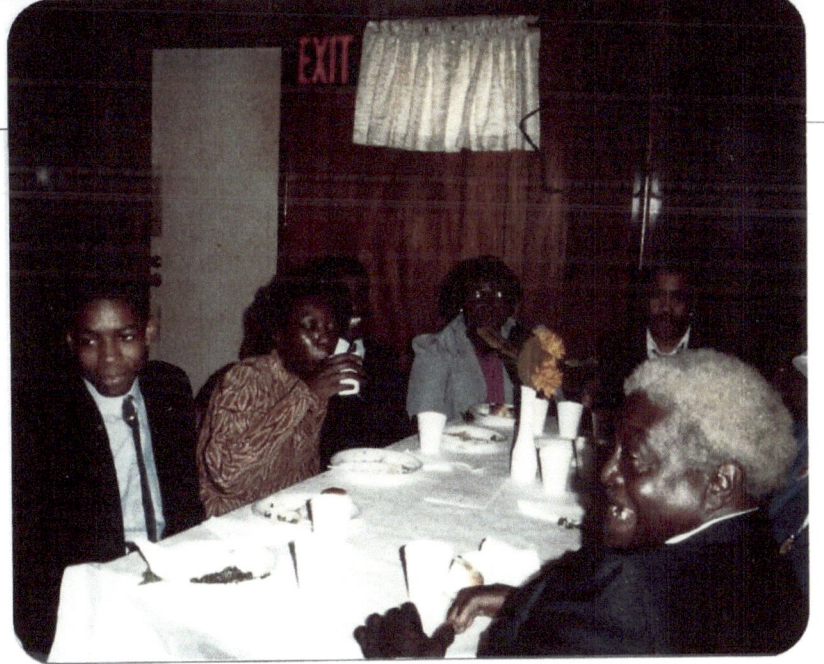

These next photos are also of Julia but her hair is braided. Her son is very young here, holding the Mickey Mouse doll, and her sister Vivian is pictured here next to Uncle George's wife, aunt Dina; wearing glasses.

My Extended Family Photos

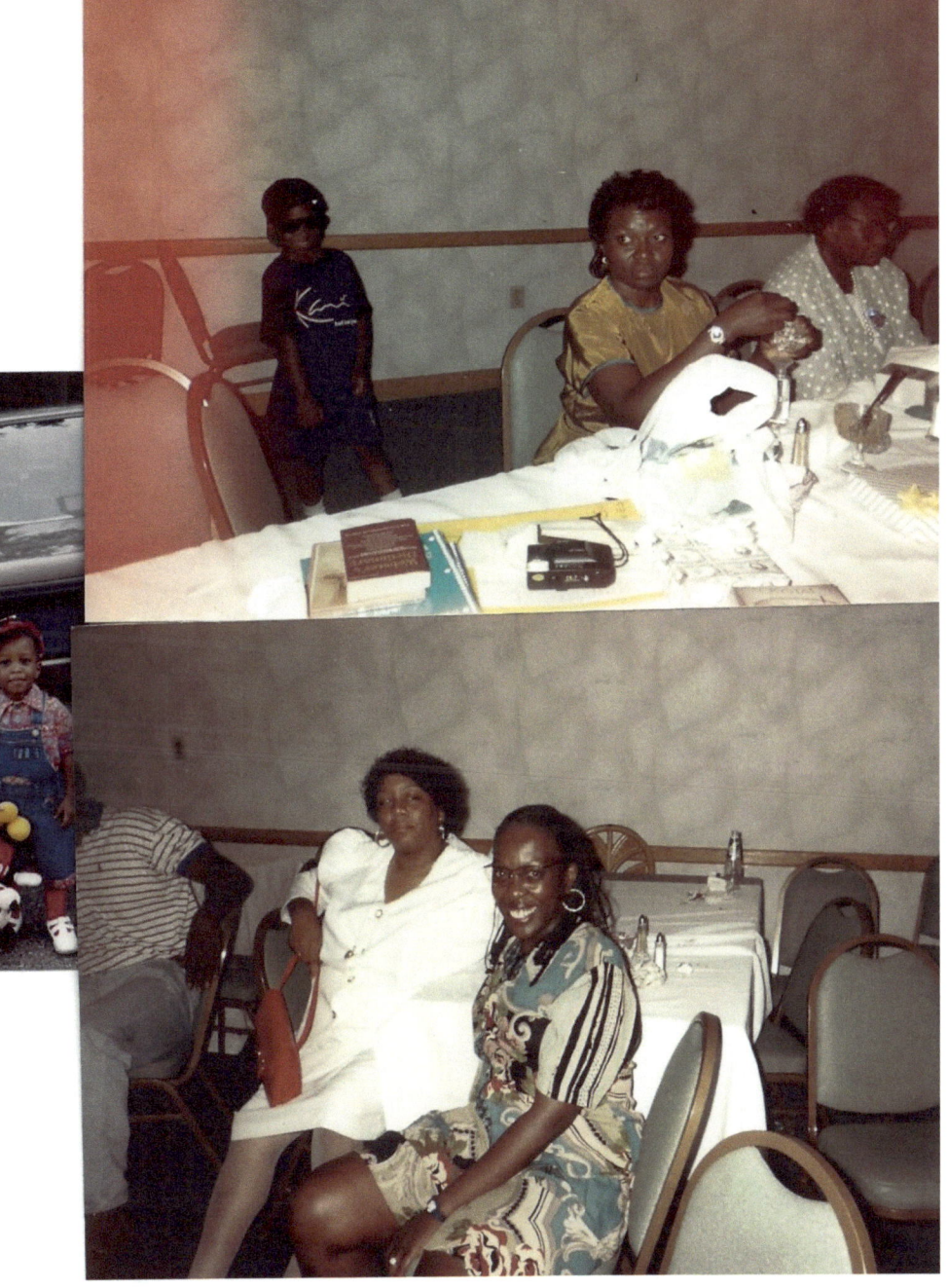

There is a photo on the next page, of my late grandfather remarrying the late Ms. Josephine many years after my grandmother passed away. Ms. Josephine already had several grown children of her own.

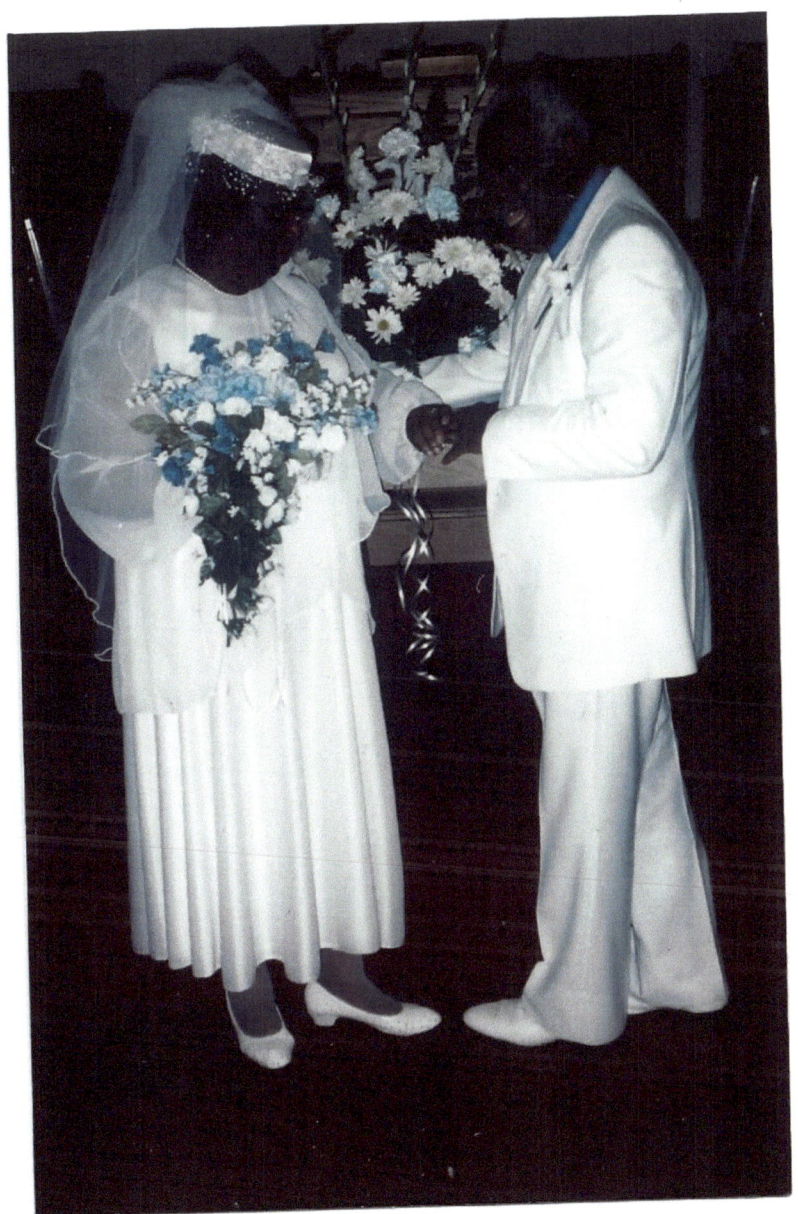

Every time I watch the movie Soul Food, I cry. My mother was the one who loved to cook and entertain. We always had a house or a yard full of family. It seemed that things changed when she passed away. Although she never had a leg removed; she did have diabetes and she used to burn her arm quite often while cooking and reaching into the oven. She never noticed it I suppose until the burn line showed up on her arm. She would prepare the dish water and me or my brother would wash the dishes. It was always way too hot. I didn't realize until it was too late that she could tolerate such hot temperatures because of her diabetes.

My Extended Family Photos

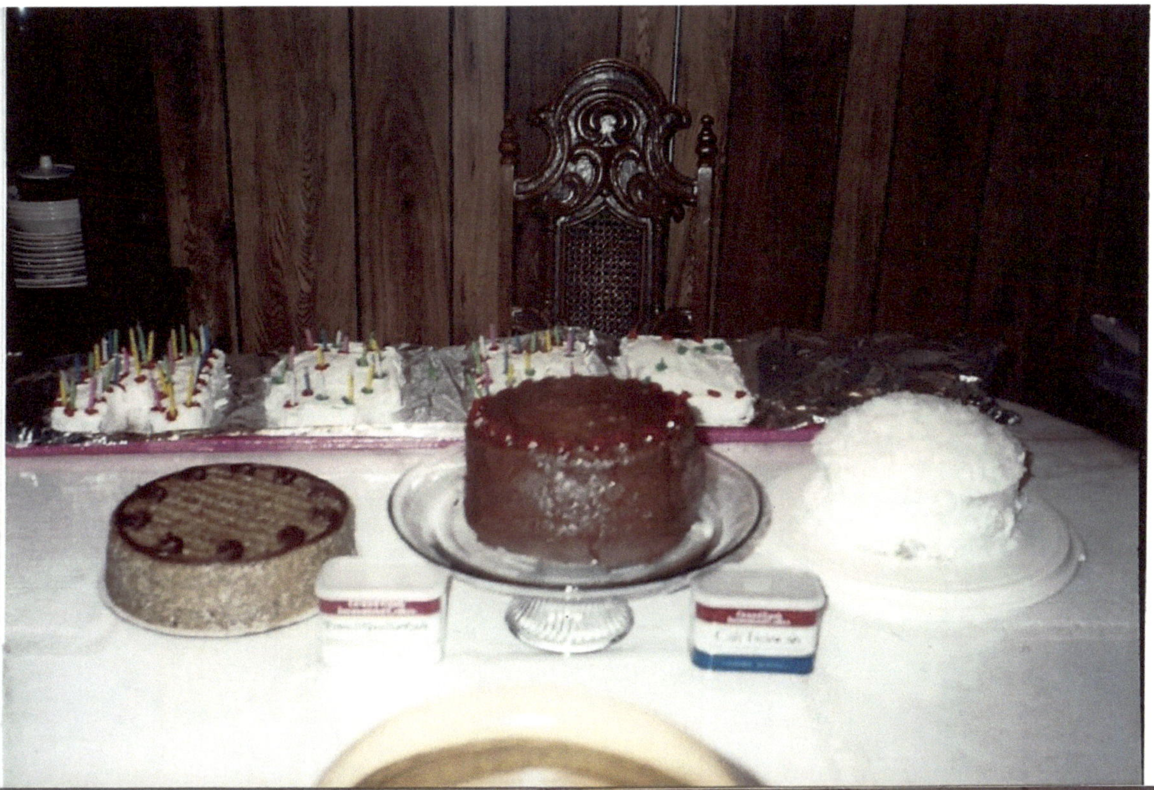

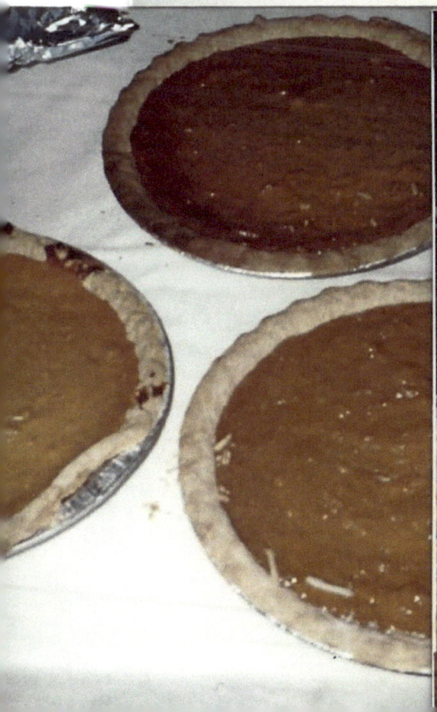

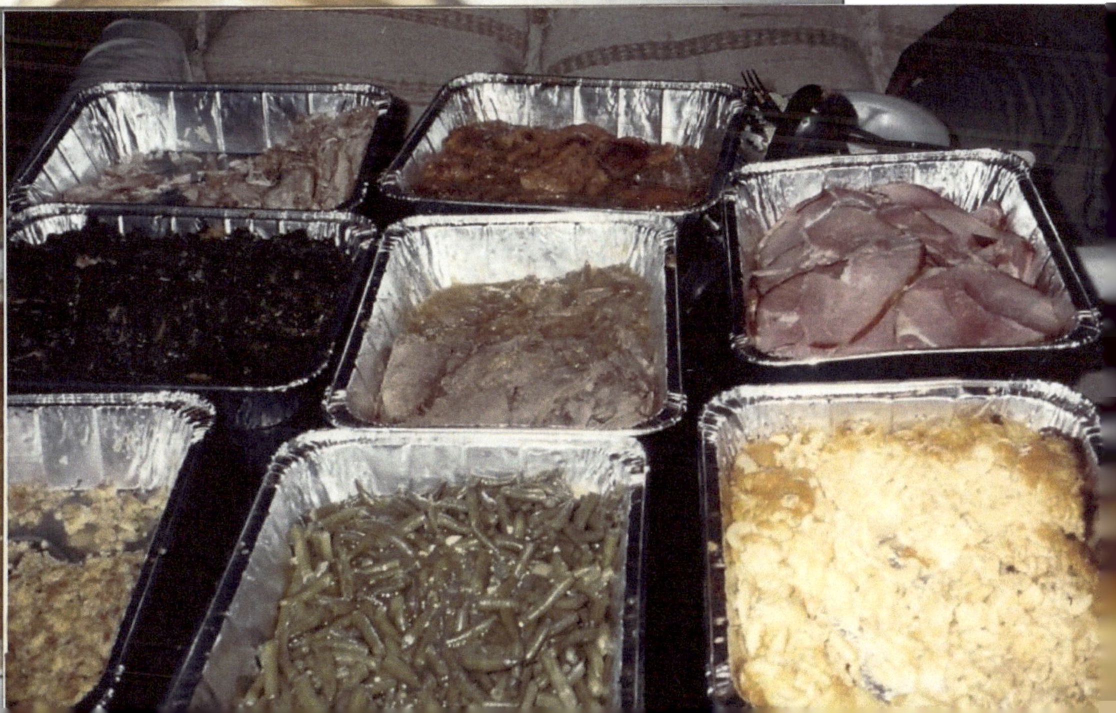

When I find out who these two lovely folks are on the following page, I will let you know.

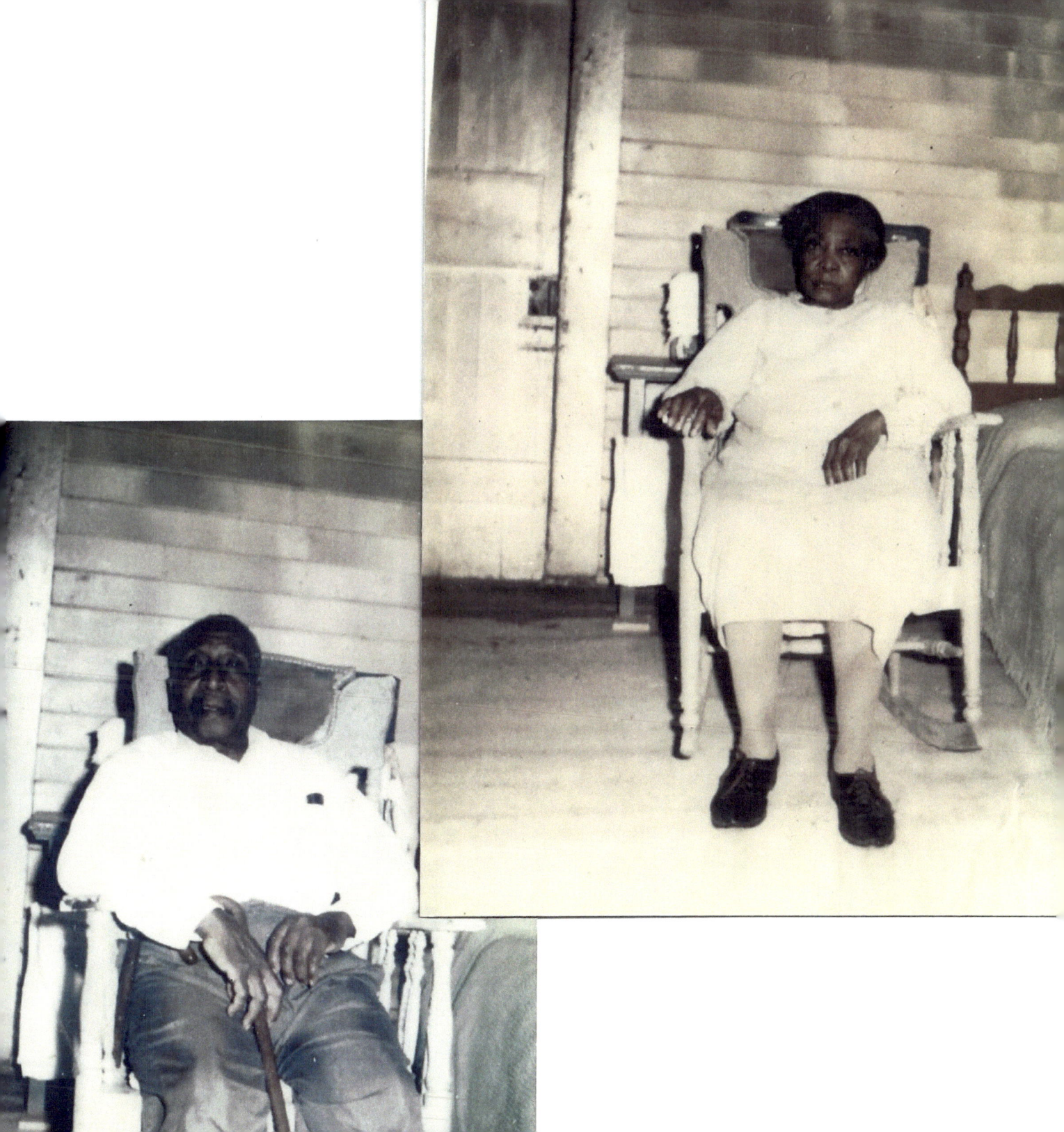

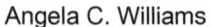

The next page is a picture of me and my daughter when she was young. The immediate family I currently live with now; (my daughter and her son Malakhi).

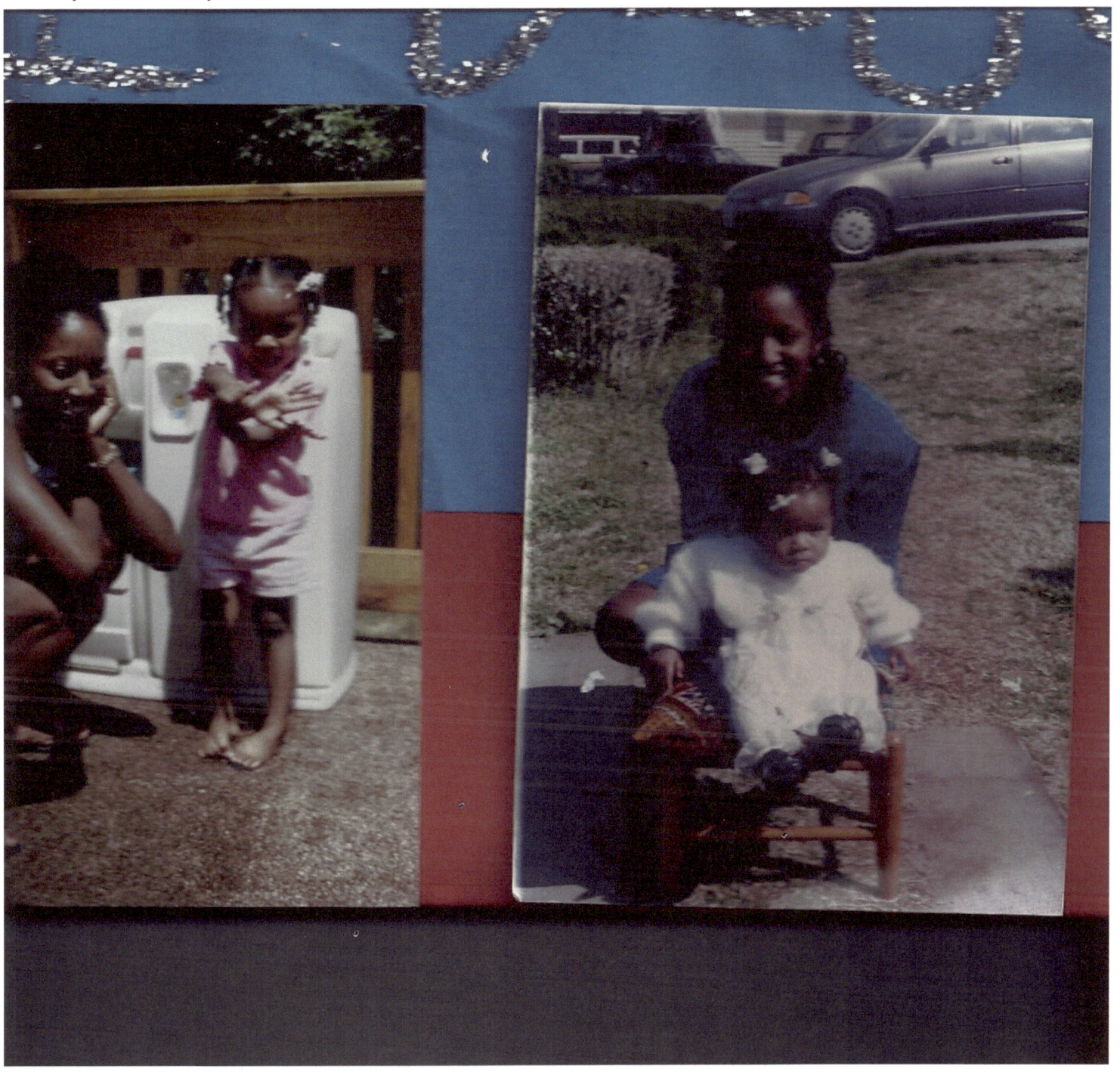

Her son's father; and me and my father; are also pictured on the following page at my grandson Malakhi's, first birthday party.

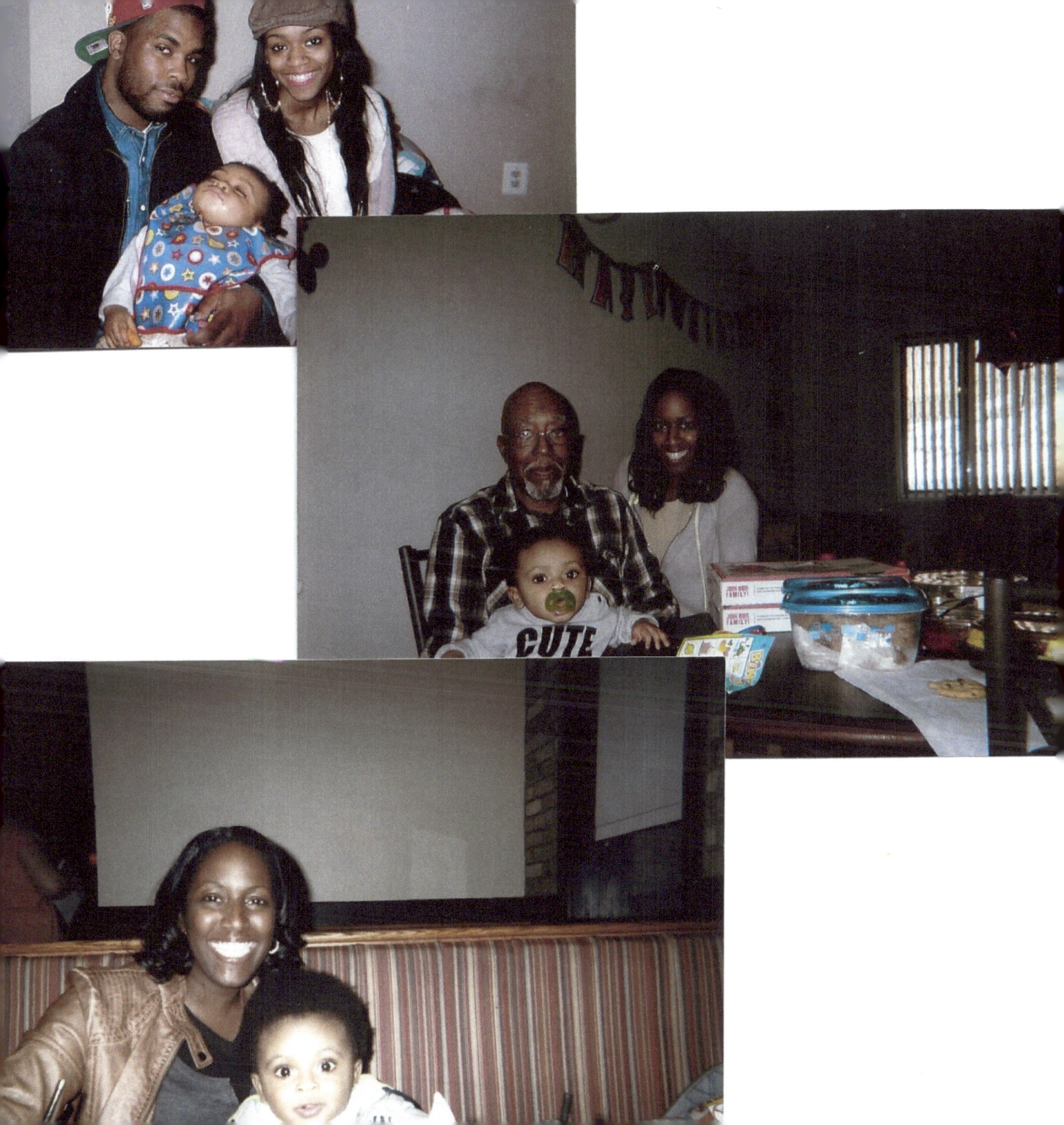

Grandpa worked hard to keep a roof over his families head for years. Although the house is not there any longer, here we are, and his house yet stands. His faithfulness to God and his enduring love for his family lives on. The sweetness that we all knew from his beautiful wife Sophonia will live on in our hearts forever. May our future (ancestors) always know just how much we loved each other.

May God continue to keep and bless us all. I Love You.

www.ingramcontent.com/pod-product-compliance
Lightning Source LLC
Chambersburg PA
CBHW040753200526
45159CB00025B/1880